I will always love you... and want to be your friend.

No matter where you're going... No matter where you've been...

Just Between Us

PAINTINGS BY

D. Morgan

HARVEST HOUSE PUBLISHERS

EUGENE, OREGON 97402

DEDICATION

To Peggy, whose unconditional friendship, spanning our lives since childhood, means more to me with each passing year. She has always been my role model for the human spirit, my confidante, and my inspiration for this book. With much love, I dedicate Just Between Us *to my dearest friend, Peggy Jones Symborski.*

Just Between Us

Copyright © 1998 Harvest House Publishers
Eugene, Oregon 97402

ISBN 1-56507-812-8

Artwork designs are reproduced under license from © Arts Uniq'®, Inc., Cookeville, TN and may not be reproduced without permission. For information regarding art prints featured in this book, please contact:

> **Arts Uniq'**
> **P.O. Box 3085**
> **Cookeville TN 38502**
> **800-223-5020**

Design and production by Garborg Design Works, Minneapolis, Minnesota

Harvest House Publishers has made every effort to trace the ownership of all poems and quotes. In the event of a question arising from the use of any poem or quote, we regret any error made and will be pleased to make the necessary correction in future editions of this book.

Manufactured in China.

98 99 00 01 02 03 04 05 06 07 / IM / 10 9 8 7 6 5 4 3 2 1

Up hill against the wind.

But never too far to travel....

.......to reach the home of a friend.

© 1995

7

No matter where you've been... No matter where you're going ~

I will always love you ~ and want to be your friend

D. Morgan © 1991.

Of all the world's wonders, none rises

to so heavenly a plane as that of a true

and lasting friendship.

SUZANNE SIEGEL ZENKEL

At my table, sit with me, I'll pour coffee or some tea.

Perhaps we'll share our tears and laughter, and be friends forever after.

D. Morgan © 1994

10

The glory of friendship is not the outstretched hand, nor the kindly smile, nor the joy of companionship; it is the spiritual inspiration that comes to one when he discovers that someone else believes in him and is willing to trust him with his friendship. My friends have come unsought. The great God gave them to me.

RALPH WALDO EMERSON

Seldom an evening is ended,

rarely a new day begins,

that I don't think about you,

good times, true love,

old friends.

D. MORGAN

I've seen the owl, I've heard the wolf.

Dear friend, I've known it all.

But your hand to bridge my troubled times

Is the sweetest to recall.

D. MORGAN

You don't know what your friendship

meant to me. I want to thank you here

and now, dear, for the warm and true

affection you've always given me.

L.M. MONTGOMERY

Anne of Avonlea

Love transcends.... everything.

D. Morgan © 1990

What would life be without a song, without a dance ~ without a little sweet romance? ~ Without a friend ~ a heart to mend? If all skies were blue above, but without Love?

..... what would life be?

D. Morgan © 1992

18

Kettles on, cups are waiting ~ favorite chairs anticipating. No matter what I have to do~ my friend, there's always time for you.

D. Morgan ©1993

23

We are kindred spirits.

D. Morgan© 1994

Thank you......

For being someone special.

D. Morgan ——— © 1991

28

There are persons so radiant, so genial, so

kind, so pleasure-bearing, that you instinctively

feel in their presence that they do you good,

whose coming into a room is like the bringing

of a lamp there.

HENRY WARD BEECHER

Friendship is a serious affection; the

most sublime of all affections,

because it is founded on principle

and cemented by time.

AUTHOR UNKNOWN